Exploring the Bible
THE DICKINSON SERIES

INTRODUCING THE OLD TESTAMENT

Leader's Guide Large Print Edition
Second Edition

Rev. Anne Robertson

MASSACHUSETTS BIBLE SOCIETY
One Book, Many Voices

Copyright © June 2013 by the Massachusetts Bible Society
Copyright © 2nd Edition 2015

All rights reserved. No part of this book may be reproduced,
stored in a retrieval system, or transmitted in any form or by any means,
electronic, mechanical, including photocopying, recording,
or otherwise, without the written permission of the publisher.

Unless otherwise indicated, Bible quotations in this book are
from the New Revised Standard Version Bible, copyright © 1989
by the National Council of Churches of Christ in the U.S.A.
Used by permission. All rights reserved.

Massachusetts Bible Society
199 Herrick Road
Newton Centre, MA 02459

Book design by Thomas Bergeron
www.thomasbergeron.com
Typeface: Jenson Pro, Gill Sans

ISBN-13: 978-0-9882481-5-1

2ND EDITION

This course is dedicated to Emily Barrett, Maybritt Muller, and all other Sunday School teachers and religious educators who have ever brought the stories of the Old Testament to life for a child.

You allowed us to stand with Daniel and experience a faith that made hungry lions lie down at our feet. You showed us that we could go against the mighty Goliaths of our lives and win. You made sure that we knew we could wrestle with God, as Jacob did, and still receive a blessing. You warned us not to be deceived by snakes in fruit trees but then assured us that our God still wanted to be with us, even when we fell for it and sinned.

Especially to Emily, Maybritt, and the Sunday School teachers of the North Scituate Baptist Church where I grew up, but also to all of you who let the great stories of an ancient faith live and breathe—thank you.

Acknowledgments

Welcome

Introducing <u>Exploring the Bible: The Dickinson Series</u>	v
Our Theological Point of View	x
Course Administration	x

Leading Exploring the Bible: The Dickinson Series

Your Students	xiii
Your Class	xxi
You Are a Facilitator	xxiv
Becoming a Registered Group Leader	xxix

Overview of Class Session Elements

Check-In	xxxi
Bible Activity	xxxii
Life Connection Activity	xxxiii
Review of Homework	xxxiii
Extra Mile Presentations	xxxiv
First and Last Sessions	xxxv

Lesson Plans

Session 1: Older Than Dirt	1
Session 2: Who's Your Daddy?	13
Session 3: Laying Down the Law	21
Session 4: United We Stand	27
Session 5: Divided We Fall	35
Session 6: Age of Empires	41

Forms, Handouts, and Supplemental Material

Form: Student Evaluation	47
Form: Facilitator Evaluation	53
Massachusetts Bible Society Statement on Scripture	57
A Covenant for Bible Study	58
Session 1 Handout: Class Contact Information	59
Session 1 Handout: Name Me, Please	61
Session 1 Handout: Is It Soup Yet?	63

Forms, Handouts, and Supplemental Material (cont.)

Session 3 Handout: The Ten Commandments	65
A Sampling of Music Resources for Session 4	67
Sample Advertising Blurbs for <u>Introducing the Old Testament</u>	69
Glossary from Student Text	70

Acknowledgments

As with the first course of <u>Exploring the Bible: The Dickinson Series</u>, I have to first acknowledge Dr. Charles Dickinson, whose gifts of time, expertise, and treasure have made this entire series possible. You can read more about him on p. vii and can watch a brief video about his hopes for this series on the website.

Given the potential minefields of approaching a text that is sacred to multiple faiths, I want to give special thanks to Dr. Marc Zvi Brettler, the Dora Professor of Biblical Studies at Brandeis University, who read through the Student Text with a particular eye toward interfaith sensitivities as well as for the accuracy of the information presented. Those interested in the Exploring the Bible series would probably also be interested in the book Dr. Brettler wrote with Dr. Peter Enns and Dr. Dan Harrington entitled <u>The Bible and the Believer: How to Read the Bible Critically and Religiously</u> (Oxford University Press, September 2012).

I also continue to be indebted to the following congregations and group facilitators who have served as pilot groups to test the effectiveness of both the Student Text and the class sessions outlined in the Leader's Guide: Dr. Ellen Porter Honnet and Jacqui James at the First Unitarian Society of Newton (West Newton, MA); Derek Kotze and Lynne Osborn at St. Matthew's United Methodist Church (Acton, MA); Aurelio Ramirez at the Lutheran Church of the Newtons (Newton, MA); Frances Taylor, Director of Faith Formation at Sacred Heart Parish (Lynn, MA); and Rev. Dr. Thomas D. Wintle at First Parish Church (Weston, MA). They had to deal with this material in its raw, unedited form, and their feedback has been critical to shaping the final product.

Our production team continues their awesome work, from editor Nancy Fitzgerald, copyeditor Jennifer Hackett, proofreader Maria Boyer, designer Thomas Bergeron, to the amazing staff I am privileged to work with at the Massachusetts Bible Society: Jocelyn Bergeron, Michael Colyott, and Frank Stevens. The MBS Trustees are also to be commended for their work in offering feedback on the materials and reaching out to find appropriate places to offer these courses.

In Gratitude,

Anne Robertson

Welcome

Welcome to the second of three courses in <u>Exploring the Bible: The Dickinson Series</u>. If you taught the first course, the format of this guide and the class sessions should be familiar to you. The basic class elements are the same, and the instructions follow the similar path of frequently dividing the class into smaller groups for discussion and comparative study.

The introductory material from the first course has been reproduced in the pages that follow for those who might be new to the series. If you did the first course, you can skim or skip these sections. However, please do review the course administration section on page x in case you have group members who might like to go on and get the Certificate of Biblical Literacy.

Whether you are new to the series or not, here are a few things to note specifically about facilitating <u>Introducing the Old Testament</u>.

- **More reading.** The Old Testament is significantly longer than the New Testament. While we don't come close to asking students to read the entire thing, there are more and longer Bible readings asked of students in this course than in the first volume. The six chapters are also longer. The Old Testament covers a time period of thousands of years. By comparison, the New Testament covers about eighty to ninety years. There is simply much more material here to cover.

Because of the expanded material, you may want to adjust your sessions depending on the makeup of your class. If your students (or you) already have relatively heavy commitments outside of this class, you might want to consider running the sessions every other week instead of every week to give enough time to digest the material.

It is not uncommon for those taking a Bible study (or any other class, for that matter!) to leave all the homework until the last minute. Your group will be best served if you discourage this early and often. Giving them two weeks between sessions won't make a bit of difference if they leave the reading to the last day.

While reading speed and comprehension vary from person to person, the average student will need about four hours to complete all of the suggested reading in a session. If they really want to think about the Reflection Questions or do the Extra Mile assignments, it could be more.

- The text references translations, issues, and concepts that were dealt with in the first course: <u>What Is the Bible?</u> Make sure your students know that relevant terms are defined in the glossary and the entire chapter from the first course relevant to the Old Testament texts is reproduced in Appendix 1 on page 177 (p. 243 LP) in the Student Text.

- The ideal group size for doing this course is eight to fifteen people. It can be successfully completed with fewer than eight, but if that is the case, you will most likely have to adjust the material. Dividing a class of eight into two groups of four works. Dividing a class of five into two groups is not nearly as effective and you will end up doing more exercises as an entire group. Since dividing the class into groups saves time, you may need longer than ninety minutes for a session if you have a smaller group that cannot be effectively divided.

- Completing the evaluations is important. We at the Massachusetts Bible Society value your feedback. These course materials are print-on-demand, which means nothing gets printed until someone orders materials. The practical result is that we can easily make changes to the materials at any time and with little cost. We look at every last word of feedback that comes in from those who use our material. When we find common threads in that feedback, we adjust either the material or our instructions accordingly. Your input makes a real difference.

Introducing Exploring the Bible: The Dickinson Series

Exploring the Bible: The Dickinson Series is a series of three, six-week courses that leads to a Certificate in Biblical Literacy from the historic Massachusetts Bible Society.

Each of the three courses is designed to fit six ninety-minute sessions with a group of eight to fifteen people. The Massachusetts Bible Society provides training, materials, and ongoing support for those who would like to run the program in their local churches or communities. Those leading the courses are not expected to be biblical experts or pastors. They are those gifted and trained to facilitate a warm, welcoming, and open group environment where the material can be presented and discussed with respect for all participants.

The Exploring the Bible Program

Three Courses: A Bird's-Eye View

I. **What Is the Bible?** A broad overview of the Bible, including chapters on how to select a Bible suitable for your needs, how the Bible is organized, how the collection of books that comprise the Bible were chosen, different ways that people approach the text, and what archaeology has to tell us about the text and its stories.

II. **Introducing the Old Testament.** A look at the best-known stories, most influential passages, and unforgettable characters that comprise the Old Testament. What are the primary themes and narratives? What are the characteristics of ancient Hebrew literature and the mindset of people in the ancient Near East? Explore both the writings themselves and the historical contexts that gave them birth.

III. **Introducing the New Testament.** Learn about Jesus as a man, as a Jewish rabbi, and as the Christ of Christian faith. Explore first-century Nazareth, what ancient letter-writing practices can tell us about Paul's letters, and the wild apocalypse of Revelation.

Online Resources

Join us for discussion on the Exploring the Bible Facebook page and follow us on Twitter @ExploreBible and swap questions and experiences with others across the country and across the world who are doing the courses in their local communities. Many of you are asking for the opportunity to take the courses online and we hope to be able to offer that down the road. And you can always check out our website at exploringthebible.org for other news, recommended reading, and to find a course near you.

The Exploring the Bible Students

The series is designed for two distinct types of students:

The Casual or Informal Students. The first group is made up of those who might know something about the Bible but have gaps in their knowledge, or those who just want to test the waters of biblical studies.

These students might want simply to take one of the three courses or put together some combination of those components without doing all that is necessary to complete the certificate program. While it's expected that this second group will still actively participate in whatever course(s) they select, there is less work expected of them outside the group setting.

The Intentional or "Extra Mile" Students. The second group represents those who have determined that they really want to do some work to build a strong foundation for Bible study. They might be Christians considering seminary, people of faith who don't know their own Scriptures very well, people of other faiths who want a clearer understanding of the Christian text, or even people of no faith who recognize the cultural and geopolitical influence of the Bible and want to understand it better. The common denominator among this group is that they want to do the whole program, including the "Extra Mile" assignments required to earn the Certificate of Biblical Literacy or Continuing Education Units (CEUs).

We hope each study group will consist of both casual and more intentional learners, and our design includes opportunities in class sessions for those engaging the material more deeply to share what they've learned with the others.

The Exploring the Bible Sponsors

The Benefactor

<u>Exploring the Bible: The Dickinson Series</u> is named in honor of its chief benefactor, Dr. Charles C. Dickinson III, a biblical scholar and long-time trustee of the Massachusetts Bible Society. Dr. Charles Dickinson was born in Charleston, West Virginia, on May 13, 1936; was educated there and at Phillips Academy, Andover, Massachusetts; and graduated cum laude in religion and philosophy from Dartmouth College, Hanover, New

Hampshire. After serving three and a half years with the US Marine Corps in the USA and Far East, he studied theology and philosophy in Chicago, Pittsburgh, West and East Germany, at Yale University, and at Union Theological Seminary in New York. He received his B.D. (Bachelor of Divinity) and Ph.D. degrees in Pittsburgh in 1965 and 1973 respectively and did post-doctoral study at Oxford University and Harvard Divinity School. Dr. Dickinson has taught in Richmond, Virginia; Kinshasa, Zaire, Congo; Charleston, West Virginia; Rome, Italy; the People's Republic of China; Andover Newton Theological School; and Beacon Hill Seminars in Boston. He lives with his wife, JoAnne, and their son, John, in Boston.

The Author

This series was conceived and designed by Rev. Anne Robertson, executive director of the Massachusetts Bible Society, who also developed and wrote the three student texts and leader's guides. She is the author of three additional books: Blowing the Lid Off the God-Box: Opening Up to a Limitless Faith (Morehouse, 2005); God's Top 10: Blowing the Lid Off the Commandments (Morehouse, 2006); and God with Skin On: Finding God's Love in Human Relationships (Morehouse, 2009). Rev. Robertson is an elder in the New England Conference of the United Methodist Church, is a winner of the Wilbur C. Ziegler Award for Excellence in Preaching, and is a sought-after speaker and workshop leader. She can be found on the web at www.annerobertson.org.

The Massachusetts Bible Society

Founded on July 6, 1809, the Massachusetts Bible Society is an ecumenical, Christian organization that has historically been a place where those across the theological spectrum of belief could unite for a common purpose. At the beginning of its history, that purpose was simply getting a copy of the Bible into the hands of anyone who wanted one, especially those without the means or opportunity to obtain one themselves. In more recent times, that work has been supplemented by the development of a variety of educational programs highlighting the importance of the Bible for faith, culture, history, and politics, as well as providing a forum for the many different voices of biblical interpretation. Exploring the Bible is a significant addition to those efforts and attempts to continue the historic tradition of being a place where those of many different faith traditions can unite for a common purpose—in this case, biblical literacy. You can find out more about the Massachusetts Bible Society at www.massbible.org.

You

Exploring the Bible: The Dickinson Series is made possible because you have elected to be a part of it. While we believe the course materials are useful in and of themselves, it is the community of students and group leaders who bring those materials to life as you engage with one another in your classes and online forums. Just by participating, you are helping to raise the level of biblical literacy in our world. You can ensure that this ministry continues by completing the facilitator and student evaluations for each course, by purchasing the materials, and by telling others about Exploring the Bible: The Dickinson Series. There are also opportunities for you to provide scholarship assistance for future students, to attend training to become a group leader, or simply to offer moral or financial support to the mission of the Massachusetts Bible Society. Our most important sponsor is you. Find out how you can help at exploringthebible.org.

Our Theological Point of View

In the creation of this series there are several obvious biases:

- The Bible is a book that can and should be read by individuals both inside and outside the church.
- Understanding of the Bible is enhanced and deepened in conversation with others.
- The tools of scholarship are not incompatible with a faithful reading of Scripture.
- Diversity of opinion is both a welcome and a necessary part of any education—especially biblical education.

Beyond those points we have tried to give an unbiased theological perspective, describing differences of opinion and scholarship in neutral terms. Although named for and written by Christians, Exploring the Bible: The Dickinson Series is designed to be an educational tool, not an evangelistic tool. The Massachusetts Bible Society affirms that the making of Christian disciples is the job of the local church. These materials are designed either to fit into the overall disciple-making effort of a local church or into a secular environment where people of other faiths or of no faith can gain a deeper understanding of the nature and content of the Bible.

Course Administration

Obtaining Credit for Certification or CEUs

Those wishing to enroll in the certificate program or obtain CEUs for their work must fill out an application and do the work in an approved small-group setting. Those who simply work their way through the materials on their own are not eligible for credit or certification.

You can find out all the details and download any necessary forms at exploringthebible.org/getting-credit.

Note that you must be a registered group leader with the Massachusetts Bible Society for any of your students to get credit. This is not difficult to obtain and is not necessary for leading an informal group. But you must register for any of your students to receive formal credit. You can find the application at exploringthebible.org/forms.

The Cost

Costs will vary depending on whether you are a casual student (which has no cost apart from the books) or are taking the course either for CEUs or certification (for which there is a fee). Please check our website at exploringthebible.org/getting-credit for more information, current rates, and information on discounts and scholarships.

Keeping in Touch

Go to exploringthebible.org to learn more or contact the Massachusetts Bible Society at 199 Herrick Road, Newton Centre, MA 02459 or dsadmin@massbible.org. You may also call us at 617-969-9404.

Note About Page References

The notation "LP" after a page number indicates the large print version of the Student Text.

Leading Exploring the Bible: The Dickinson Series

(Note: Some people contact the Massachusetts Bible Society in search of someone who would lead a group in their location. If you would be interested in such an opportunity, please contact us.)

Your Students

The Exploring the Bible student materials can be used by anyone, whether they're part of a formal class or not. It's designed, however, for a group of eight to fifteen adults to study together, and students will gain the most from the series if they participate in such a group. You may be part of a church or other organization that has recruited you to facilitate the class, or you may have just picked up the materials on your own and decided that you wanted to lead a group in your community. Either way, there are things to think about when putting a group together.

Who Would Be Interested in This Course?

There are three groups of people whose interest might be piqued by this series:

First are those for whom it is primarily designed: People who know little to nothing about the Bible and its contents. They don't know Adam from Abraham from Jesus and couldn't name a Bible story if you paid them. They might be Christians seeking knowledge of their own sacred text, members of another religion who want to learn about the Bible, or those of no particular faith at all who simply recognize the cultural, historical, and social impact of the Bible on world civilization. What they have in common is that, for all intents and purposes, they have never cracked open a Bible. Especially if they are Christians in a church, this group may be embarrassed to admit their degree of biblical illiteracy.

Second, there are many, many people who know a good bit about the contents of the Bible but next to nothing about the context of the Bible—for example, how it was put together and when, the history and culture of biblical times, and so on. This second group may also find a great benefit in Exploring the Bible: The Dickinson Series because of the inclusion of that type of information in the materials and exercises.

Third, there are (for want of a better term) Bible study "junkies." Found mostly (although not exclusively) in churches, these folks will sign up for anything at all with the Bible in the title on the off chance that there may still be some teensy bit of biblical information they're lacking.

Each of these groups can find some benefit in the study—no matter how much you already know about the Bible there is always more to learn, especially as you discuss passages with others. Problems may arise, however, when the various knowledge levels are grouped together, because the questions and issues that come up are qualitatively different for each type of group.

For example, groups two and three might start comparing this Bible text to another while group one is still trying to figure out who the characters in the story are. As the discussions move on without them, referencing stories and texts with which the first group is entirely unfamiliar, the first group starts to feel dumb and drops out, and you lose the very type of student the course is designed to help.

With some finesse and discussion control by the facilitator, the first two types of students can be mixed in the same class without too many difficulties (although ideally there would be one group of pure neophytes and a second group of those lacking only the contextual piece). The third group, however, really needs to be actively discouraged from taking the class as a student, unless the whole class has substantial knowledge. Otherwise they will almost certainly hinder learning in others.

I have seen this time and time again in groups designed for beginning Bible students. The junkies come, monopolize the discussions, and soon the real neophytes are dropping out with an apologetic, "Oh, I thought this was just for new people." Your Bible junkies should be encouraged to facilitate a class themselves or, if there are enough of them, a class could be made up of just this type of student. They also could be encouraged to simply read the materials on their own.

If the person absolutely cannot be dissuaded from attending (or if to do so will cause too much conflict), consider giving them some sort of title or special advisory role in the group—perhaps as a co-facilitator. This will at least keep other students from feeling embarrassed about their knowledge by comparison.

Getting the Right People Together

The key to having groups that are basically on the same level of Bible knowledge is both in your initial advertising and in your follow-up with those who express an interest. At the end of this guide on page 69 are some advertising blurbs you can use to announce the course and solicit interest. You can also, of course, write your own. To avoid the pitfalls of mixing incompatible Bible knowledge levels, it will be most helpful if your advertising asks people to contact you (or whoever is receiving the information) in order to "express interest" rather than "sign up." That gives you the opportunity for a follow-up conversation in which you can find out the person's relative level of biblical knowledge and make appropriate recommendations.

In gauging the level, don't give an impromptu Bible pop-quiz; just ask something along these lines: "We like to put together groups of people with similar levels of knowledge about the Bible. A lot of people—even in churches—really don't know the Bible at all, others know a number of the stories but don't really know how the Bible itself was put together or they may struggle in reading it. Still others have taken lots of Bible studies and are eager to know even more. Do you see yourself in any of those groups? Why are you interested in this course?"

A conversation like that allows you to let people know the parameters of whatever group is set up without sounding like you are giving anyone preferential treatment. Some possible responses to your callers' comments: "Gosh, Sarah, the only people who responded are those who don't even have a basic knowledge of the Sunday School stories. We have enough for that group but we didn't get enough for a group at your level of knowledge. We might even have enough for two of those basic groups. Would you possibly be interested in leading one?" Or, "Well, Zach, we have enough for a group, but most of them have a lot more experience with the Bible than you do. You're more than welcome to come to the class if you're comfortable with that—after all, the material was designed for those who haven't even cracked the book—or you can wait for another group. It's your call."

Ideally you should establish the dates and times for the class and begin advertising for students two to three months before the time of the first class, maybe more if you're part of a busy organization that schedules events six months to a year out. Give people enough time to get the dates on their calendars so that you can ensure the best attendance possible.

Advertise the course in places where the students you want to attract will see it. If you represent a church that wants to reach out into the community with this course, advertising only in the church bulletin or on the church website will not help you achieve your goal. And don't forget to mention the class on social media. If you are open to people outside of your church or community attending your class, go to exploringthebible.org to list your class for those who might be looking for a venue near them.

Opening Up to the Community

The Massachusetts Bible Society often hears from people who are looking for a Bible study course in their area. Because Exploring the Bible offers Continuing Education Units (CEUs) and a certificate program (for those who do the Extra Mile work in the Student Text), we would like to know if you'd be willing to accept student referrals from the Massachusetts Bible Society for your group.

If so, we'll be glad to post the details of your class on our website to let interested parties know where they can find a course and we will advertise your course to our e-mail list. To make this manageable for you, please be sure to set a registration deadline and send the information to us as soon as you know it.

We also receive occasional requests from churches or other organizations that would like to run a course but don't have a leader. If you would be willing to facilitate the course for others, please drop us a line and let us know.

Students Who Miss a Class

Class dates, times, and locations should be established far enough in advance that students can plan their schedules in a way that minimizes conflicts with other activities. From your initial contact with potential students onward, the importance of attending class, both for themselves and for others in the class, should be stressed.

Even so, scheduling conflicts will come up and students will miss classes from time to time. Those seeking CEUs or the full Certificate in Biblical Literacy may miss one class, if necessary. The homework from the missed session, however, still must be completed. Those informal students who would like a completion certificate for this one course may miss up to two classes.

If students are missing more than two sessions, they are missing at least half the course and it's worth asking them whether they would like to simply wait and take it at a time that's better for them. Every person who attends enhances the learning of others in the class. Those who miss classes are not just missing an opportunity for their own education but are hampering the ability of others to have the full group experience.

If a student wants to make up a class, that is solely up to you as the group leader. If you want to take the extra time, that's your call. It is not necessary.

It is helpful for you to have a backup leader, however, in case you have to miss a class for any reason.

Students Who Don't Do Homework

Your initial contact with potential students should include the information that there will be homework in the course—to a greater or lesser degree, depending on the level of recognition they are seeking. **The homework for informal students ranges from about twenty minutes to two and a half hours per week, depending on the session and the course. Extra Mile students can count on several hours each week.**

As with class attendance, the expectations are greater for those seeking CEUs or certification. Continuing Education Units and progress toward the full Certificate in Biblical Literacy will only be granted when all the regular and Extra Mile homework has been completed and not more than one class session has been missed. Completion certificates for informal students will only be granted when the facilitator verifies that the student has come to class prepared and has not missed more than two sessions.

You will, most likely, have at least a couple of students who simply don't complete the reading assignments, week after week. Sessions are designed so that even these students should be able to get something out of the class session. Be sure your students realize that it's better to come to class unprepared than not to come at all. They can still learn—they just won't have as rich an experience as they would otherwise.

If you notice that very few are able to complete the reading, you might consider holding sessions less frequently—perhaps every other week instead of every week, for example. Courses two and three have considerably more reading than course one, and if you have participants with busy lives they might appreciate a longer time frame. Of course if they are still just going to wait until the night before to try to cram it all in, having a longer stretch will not help.

Some reminders are built into the curriculum. The last element of every class session is a review of the homework for the coming week. You might also want to send an e-mail midweek to jog your students' memory—perhaps with a teaser from one of the questions for reflection in the Student Text. If someone has posted on the Exploring the Bible Facebook page, you could also send a brief e-mail notice inviting students to check out the new thread or new response.

Don't make a spectacle of or chide students who frequently are not prepared, especially in front of others. It's often helpful, however, to have a private conversation with such a student to see what the issues are that are preventing the work from being done. You might be able to offer some solutions or guidance. Remember the great caveat of Plato: "Be kind, for everyone is fighting a great battle." When your students finally meet God face to face, nobody is going to be asking them why they didn't do their Exploring the Bible homework. Keep perspective.

Dealing with Problem Personalities

One of the most difficult parts of leading any group, no matter what the topic, is the truly problem personality. While everyone can have a bad day and some people have quirks that can cause awkward moments, sometimes you'll run across participants who prevent the group from accomplishing its goals. They might consistently dominate the discussion and pull the group off track, make comments that are offensive and/or threatening, or exhibit other behaviors that either destroy the open and inclusive atmosphere or make getting through the material impossible.

If you should end up with "that guy" or "that gal" in your group and repeated attempts at (private) correction have not yielded a change in behavior, please talk either with your pastor or the Massachusetts Bible Society to resolve the issue. In rare cases a person might have to be asked to leave the group. And whatever you do, make sure you don't become "that guy" or "that gal"!

Your Class

Group Size

The session activities in this Leader's Guide assume a group size of eight to fifteen people. Sessions often call for the students to be divided into smaller groups for discussion. This both saves time and allows those who are reticent to speak up in a larger group to still have input and express their views.

This course will be challenging to do with fewer than eight students. Over the course of the study, someone will get sick, someone will suddenly be without transportation, someone's child will have a recital, someone will get called in to work, and you will find yourself trying to do a session with two students. Without a rich and varied discussion in class, students are not receiving the full benefit of the course, even if they are one of the two students who did show up. If you cannot recruit a class of at least eight students, consider rescheduling the course for another time or make sure you really have an attendance commitment from the ones you have.

If your church is small, consider reaching out to other churches in your area. These courses have been used successfully with both ecumenical and interfaith groups as well as groups that include atheists and agnostics. Think beyond the walls of your church or organization.

This course will be difficult to do with more than fifteen students. And fifteen is pushing it. This is a small-group study. With more than fifteen students it is easy to lose the intimacy that allows for the trust, bonding, and sharing that make small groups such a powerful learning environment. You will also be hard-pressed to keep within the session time frame of ninety minutes. If you have more than fifteen who are interested, consider dividing them into two classes.

If you have a large group and five or more are Extra Mile students (see p. vii), you might also consider having one class of only those more intentional learners. Since they cannot receive the certificate or CEUs without full completion of the course (see p. x), you are less likely to have attendance issues in that group.

As you progress beyond Course One in the series, you may have new students who have not taken the previous courses. This is especially true of the New Testament course, since many Christians tend to think the Old Testament is irrelevant and might skip the first courses to wait for the "real Bible." Our evaluations have shown that sometimes this has been a hurdle for the new students. The early courses give some important background both on the Bible itself and on the overall purpose and approach of the course. And, of course, a solid understanding of the Old Testament is critical for a proper understanding of the New.

While there is no need to forbid students to jump in to a later course if they haven't done the early ones, you should let them know that others who have done so have not gotten the same benefit as those who took the courses in order. You could also encourage such students to get the student books for the other courses to read in preparation.

Meeting Location

Your meeting space can either help or hinder the students' learning and will send unconscious messages about how open people should be about their thoughts and circumstances. While this is a class for which some students will receive various kinds of credit, a classroom atmosphere of students lined up in rows (or pews) in front of a teacher will not be ideal. Students should be in a setting where they can easily see one another as well as the facilitator, can engage in discussions (either in one group or in sub-groups), can enjoy refreshments without worry, and can sit for an hour and a half without discomfort.

Be sure to look for a space that can accommodate students with mobility issues or other types of disabilities. Remember that each course's Student Text is available in both regular and large print.

If you're leading a group in which everyone is familiar with one another and you're not accepting any referral students, then meeting in someone's home is ideal. If you're a church group, meeting in a home means you don't have to worry that six other groups want the church lounge the same night you want it, and the home atmosphere can make people feel…well…at home. Do be sure, however, that it is a home that, at least for that time, will be relatively free of distractions and that it can comfortably accommodate the number of people in your group.

If you want to draw in some new folks to your group, it's better to find a public location. This might be the aforementioned church lounge, a library or community center with available meeting space, or your local pub or coffee shop. As the group gets to know one another, you might decide to move elsewhere, but at the outset meet at a location that group members can easily find and get to.

Don't discount the possibility of hosting the class at another institution. Want students from the nearby college? Call the chaplain and see about getting space for the class on campus. Want to help seniors at the local assisted-living facility keep their minds active? See if you can use space right there. Does your congregation have an active prison outreach? Teach it there. A good host is always planning for the ease and comfort of the guests. Model biblical hospitality in your meeting space.

You Are a Facilitator

Many people feel intimidated by the thought of leading a Bible study. There is the perception that to lead people through a study of the Bible, one must be a learned biblical scholar or a pastor. That would be true if the course leader were developing the materials to be taught. With Exploring the Bible, however, the Massachusetts Bible Society has provided material that is grounded in solid biblical scholarship but that can be presented by those without specific biblical training. As a group leader, you are a facilitator, not a teacher. The information is in the books, you are just there to help people find their way through it.

Of course there's nothing wrong with having a biblical scholar or pastor lead this course. It is simply our belief that such qualification is not necessary to effectively introduce students to the Bible. You can do this!

But I Don't Know the Answers!

Undoubtedly there will be class sessions in which questions arise that aren't addressed in the Student Text or Leader's Guide. When that happens and you don't know the answer, don't panic. You're not in this alone. Let's review your options for dealing with questions that stump you. Whatever option you choose, please be sure to record the question.

If the same question keeps popping up in different groups, we'll know we should address it in a revision of the Student Text.

- If the question is specific to a particular Bible passage, ask students to look in the notes associated with that passage in their study Bibles. Ask: "Does anyone have notes that address the question?" This approach helps students familiarize themselves with how a study Bible can help them.

- If your meeting location has wi-fi access or a tech-savvy student has a smart phone, type the question into Google and see what comes up. This can help students see how to research their own questions when they arise outside a class setting. There are new Bible study tools appearing online all the time. You can find a listing of some we find helpful at www.massbible.org/how-to-study-bible.

- Suggest that someone submit the question to the Ask-a-Prof service of the Massachusetts Bible Society. This is a free service and can be found at www.massbible.org/ask-a-prof.

- Encourage students to "like" the Exploring the Bible Facebook page to discuss their questions with students in other groups and the Massachusetts Bible Society staff.

- Volunteer to research the question yourself and bring back a response the next week. In doing that research, you can ask other members of your church, check the Internet or library, or contact the Massachusetts Bible Society for a response.

- Remind students that not all questions have "answers" per se. Sometimes a variety of opinions will be the best you can do. Be sure students know that Appendix 5 on page 201 (p. 271 LP) in their Student Text suggests resources for finding answers to their questions.

Atmosphere Is Everything

Learning is more than absorbing a set of facts. To truly learn and grow, students must feel that their honest questions are taken seriously and that they won't be judged for expressing their opinions. Perhaps the most important role of the group leader is ensuring that the class environment is "safe" in that regard. Students are willing to take risks in learning when they feel a class environment is safe.

This course was not created as a tool for Christian evangelism and faith formation, although the Massachusetts Bible Society is certainly not opposed to such activities. With Exploring the Bible, however, we wanted to create a vehicle in which people of all faiths or no faith could learn more about the Bible for any and all reasons. We believe that faith formation is the role of the local church. What we have provided in Exploring the Bible is an educational tool that can be used to anchor that faith formation in local churches and to provide information about the Bible that can be accepted in secular and interfaith settings.

To make that possible, the class setting and atmosphere must work to embrace not only very, very basic questions (for example, "Is 'Christ' Jesus' last name?") with respect, but must also be open to those who might challenge traditional Christian interpretations or express dislike for biblical passages. Even if you have an entire group of professing Christians, there are probably beliefs and opinions in the room that contradict Christian orthodoxy or run afoul of the doctrines of a particular tradition or denomination. As long as the question is sincere and isn't coming from a problem personality purposely trying to stir the pot, your job is to make sure that the person asking feels heard and respected and that the question is given a fair hearing.

How the first such question is handled will determine the extent of real learning that can occur. Being able to hear challenging questions and comments without bristling is a much more important qualification for being a leader of these courses than Bible knowledge. Of course any statements that demean another race, gender, sexual orientation, or anything else should be swiftly corrected and apologized for.

Should the Leader Participate?

In most cases, the person leading the class should not participate as a class member in the exercises, even if you are learning the material along with the students. Any one of the exercises during class sessions could easily take up the entire class time. You're needed as a timekeeper and cannot fulfill that role as effectively if you're involved in discussion yourself. You should, however, be completely familiar with the exercise that the class is doing and with the material on which it's based. A thorough checklist for class preparation is provided at the beginning of each session's lesson plan.

You're also in a role of authority, even if you don't feel particularly authoritative. For some students, when the leader weighs in on a subject (especially when that leader is also a pastor or other respected person in the community), it can come across as pressure to conform to that leader's opinion. When that occurs, learning is stunted, since it may be perceived that not all opinions or positions can be freely considered.

That's not to say you must always remain silent and aloof. There may be an occasion when you need to participate for reasons of group cohesion. If, for example, a class has a member with a difficult personality who is making discussion in smaller groups difficult, you might volunteer to be that person's partner for one of the exercises. You should also step in to help de-escalate any conflicts, to protect those expressing unpopular opinions, to prod a stalled discussion, or to get a discussion back on track.

If group members are asking for your opinion, try to dissuade them or at least give your opinion last so that others don't feel constrained from expressing different thoughts. And even then, tread with caution. The authority figure speaking last can seem to negate or even mock all different responses that have been given prior. If you must weigh in, do so last and with a huge dose of humility and respect for other opinions expressed. When you can affirm any part of what someone else thinks, do so.

The only time more intentional participation might be warranted is if you end up with a group that is thinking rigidly and as a monolith. If there are no divergent opinions in the group, something is amiss either in class atmosphere or in student imagination. There are always differences of opinion among human beings, even if the people are part of the same faith tradition or even the same church.

If those alternative opinions are not being expressed, it's part of your job to break down whatever walls are keeping them out. That might involve you throwing out some different ideas for discussion, even if they're not opinions that you favor. Just keep your disfavor to yourself and encourage a discussion of the ideas on their own merits. That will help students to see that the expression of different opinions is not only safe but also encouraged and will help them learn to think outside the box.

Please Give Us Feedback

Near the back of this guide are course evaluations for both students and group leaders. Every Student Text has that same course evaluation in it and you can find it online at exploringthebible.org/forms. It is so helpful to us to receive these evaluations. The lesson plan for Session 6 includes time for evaluation and provides instructions for returning evaluations to us. Because these courses are being published in a print-on-demand format, we can make adjustments to the text very easily.

Whether you are letting us know about a typo that we missed or letting us know the ways that the course did or didn't work for you and your group, your feedback helps us to make this material the best it can be. We read every single evaluation that comes to us and while we love to hear praise and sometimes use those statements for testimonials, we truly want to know if something about the course material or presentation has been problematic. If the same criticisms keep coming across the desk, we fix the problem.

Please let us hear from you. It really helps.

Becoming a Registered Group Leader

If you just have informal students in your group, then there is no need to register with the Massachusetts Bible Society. If you have Extra Mile students who are seeking credit, however, they can only get that credit with a registered group leader. It isn't hard to register, but it is necessary for anyone in your group to get formal credit for their work.

To register, go to exploringthebible.org/forms and you will find two documents. One is the actual Application to Lead Groups for Credit and the other is the document that spells out the details of working with students seeking credit. The latter document is under "Other Documents of Interest" on the Forms page and is called "Expectations and Requirements for Leading a Group for Credit." Read that and send us the application.

If you have any questions, feel free to call or e-mail us.

Overview of Class Session Elements

Check-In

Beginning in Session 2, each class session begins with a set of two check-in questions about the material to be dealt with in that session:

- What is one thing I have learned from this material?
- What is one question I have related to this week's topic?

These questions are posed in the Student Text to help participants prepare for the next class, so ideally they have already thought about them. **These are not designed to be discussion questions. Responses should be one or two sentences at most, simply stated by students without any elaboration.** It's simply a way to gauge where students are and to allow participants to hear, in their classmates' responses, questions or issues they may not have thought about themselves. It is also a helpful tool to get people focused on the material at hand and to remember some of the themes and stories they read about.

One way to assure that check-in time doesn't turn into a full-blown discussion is to simply record the responses on your white board or newsprint or on paper. That way, questions won't get lost in the shuffle and if there isn't a sufficient response during the rest of the class session it can be carried over or addressed through one of the means discussed in the "But I Don't Know the Answers" section on page xxiii. **This technique of writing questions to be answered later is often called the "Parking Lot"—a place to park your questions and issues for a bit to see if they're answered by later activity.**

Bible Activity

Most sessions contain a thirty-minute activity that examines a particular biblical passage or story in detail. The goal of this activity is to become more familiar with a well-known Bible story or passage and to get some practice thinking critically about the text. Students will be divided into two or more groups and encouraged to use the resources in their study Bibles as well as the text itself.

For some students, this program will represent an entirely new way of looking at the Bible and could be unsettling at times, depending on their background. Go gently in such instances and respect the struggles some might have in, for example, finding that the creation stories in Genesis 1 and Genesis 2–3 don't match. Don't rush to find solutions, but don't dismiss student concerns, either. You may want to ask some students to formulate their concerns into questions or issues that can be put in the Parking Lot to see if further light is shed along the way.

The Bible Activity is usually wrapped up with groups reporting back in some way about what they've discovered in their study of the text.

Life Connection Activity

Most sessions also contain a thirty-minute activity on a second well-known passage of the Bible. The difference is that in this activity the questions are more reflective. Here the objective is to explore the ways in which the Bible has relevance in daily life—either in the individual life of the student or in the broader scope of community and culture.

When students are asked to reflect more personally about a Bible passage, the groups are typically smaller (two to three people) so that it's a bit easier to open up to someone else. These responses are typically not conveyed to the group at large but are left in the sharing of the small groups.

In both the Bible and Life Connection Activities, students will learn more if they're with different groups each week. Encourage students to group with those they haven't before and recommend that couples and close friends split up into different pairs or groupings for these exercises. If there is great reluctance to do this, it need not be forced, but do keep trying for new group permutations.

Review of Homework

The Student Text contains homework—one assignment for all students and a second assignment for those seeking certification or CEUs. The latter are referred to as the Extra Mile students, and in order to earn their certification, they must complete **both** sets of homework. At the end of each session, spend about five minutes looking over the homework for the next session to resolve any questions and to offer a constant reminder that there is homework to be done.

Extra Mile Presentations

To be sure that those who have chosen to engage in more in-depth study of the material don't feel they're simply jumping through hoops for their certification, several of the sessions include a fifteen-minute period for those who have done this extra work to present what they've learned. Depending on the number of Extra Mile students in your group, this will require some judgment calls on your part to keep to the time frame.

Not every session includes an Extra Mile presentation. When the Extra Mile work has been personal and reflective, sharing of these assignments has not been included so that students might feel freer in their expression. The presentations are suggested, however, when the homework has included extra research on a topic related to the subject of the particular session.

Please make private notes about these presentations that briefly answer the following questions:

- **Who made a presentation?**
- **Did the presentation reflect that the assignment had been done?**
- **Any other notes you believe would be helpful in judging whether the student has done the appropriate level of work for the extra recognition they are to receive.**

While the Extra Mile work is required for certification and CEUs, others are welcome to do these exercises if they wish. If they do, they should be encouraged to share their findings along with the others. Be sure to keep the same set of notes for these students as well, just in case they decide at some point during the course to go for the certificate or CEUs.

At the conclusion of the course, these private notes should be submitted to the Massachusetts Bible Society to help with student evaluation. Most of the Extra Mile assignments include some written work. Students should keep these in a folder and submit them to the Massachusetts Bible Society at the conclusion of the course.

If you have a group (or a particular session) with no Extra Mile students, give the extra time to one or more of the other session activities.

First and Last Sessions

The first session of each course includes elements to help the group begin to get to know each other and lay the groundwork for future class sessions. There is some kind of icebreaker, a review of the nature and scope of the series, and guidelines for establishing a Bible study covenant.

It is always helpful if students can get books ahead of the first class and begin reading, but there are many reasons why that might not be possible. The exercises in the first session always assume that students have not read the first session of the Student Text. These exercises will have students actively using their student books more than in later sessions, where they will use the Bible more than their Student Texts.

The last session of each course is also a bit different. There is time in these lesson plans for both oral and written evaluation, celebration of the students' achievement, presentation of certificates, and housekeeping issues. The exercises in these sessions often reflect back on the course as a whole.

There are two kinds of certificates for each course. Informal students get a Certificate of Participation. These are available at exploringthebible.org/forms for you to download, fill out, and give directly to your students.

Extra Mile students get a Certificate of Completion. These must be requested from the Massachusetts Bible Society. You are prompted to send the information to us at the conclusion of session four so that there will be time to process these certificates and get them to you for the final session.

Lesson Plan

OLDER THAN DIRT

Objectives

- To introduce students to one another and to the course.
- To familiarize students with two foundational stories from the oldest period of the Bible.
- To help students recognize the differences between our contemporary mindset and the worldview of the ancient Near East.

Materials Needed

- Nametags
- Bibles, newsprint and stand, whiteboard, or other means of posting information before students
- Markers (for the appropriate surface)
- Several study Bibles in different translations and with different perspectives

Handouts

- Name Me, Please (p. 61). You will need one for each student. (While this is available at the end of this guide in black and white, some might prefer to download the full-color version from exploringthebible.org/forms and make color copies.)
- Is It Soup Yet? (p. 65). You will need one for every 3-4 people in your class.
- Class Contact Information form (p. 59). You will need just one copy to circulate.

Leader Preparation

- Read the introductory portions of this guide as well as the student text through the end of Session 1.
- Become familiar with the texts and activities for the Session 1 class session.
- Find and prepare needed materials and handouts.
- Write out the questions in Part II of the Life Connection Activity so that group members can easily see them while they discuss.

Gathering

The initial class announcement should invite students to come ten to fifteen minutes before the actual start of the ninety-minute session. During this time, each student should receive a nametag and their Student Text (if not procured ahead of time). It is always a nice gesture to have simple refreshments available. Make sure students add their contact information to the Class Contact list, and be sure to determine which, if any, of the students will be doing the class for certification or CEUs.

Make sure students are aware of the following regarding their contact information:

- During the course the information will be used by the group leader to contact students about course matters.
- Unless otherwise indicated, contact information will be shared with the Massachusetts Bible Society at the end of the course.
- The Massachusetts Bible Society will not share that information with any third party.
- Students will then receive one e-mail from the Massachusetts Bible Society to determine how much and what kind of contact a student would like to receive going forward. These options might include:
  - *Being a part of the regular Massachusetts Bible Society mailing list*
  - *Receiving information related to future Exploring the Bible courses, conferences, or activities*
  - *Receiving all event notifications from the Massachusetts Bible Society*

Session 1 Activities

Icebreaker: Name Me, Please
(12 Min)

Part I *(6 min)*

- Welcome the group, give your own name, and ask students to pair up with someone they don't know or don't know well.

- Give each student a copy of the handout, Name Me, Please. Read the short paragraph at the top of the handout and explain that each pair has six minutes to come up with names for each of the creatures pictured. (Make sure students understand that, while these are all actual species, you are not asking them to provide the established name. They are playing Adam and should invent their own name for each creature.)

- During this exercise, each person should also learn the name of his or her partner.

- Ask each pair to select a reporter to share their results with the larger group.

Part II *(6 min)*

- Bring the pairs back into the larger group and have each reporter share his or her own name, the name of his or her partner, and the names they devised for their three creatures.

- You may then share the three actual names of the creatures: the long-eared jerboa, the albino tawny frogmouth owl, and the sea lamprey.

Notes

Session 1 Activities

Notes

Group Covenant and Series Information (13 Min)

Refer students to pages vii-xi (p. viii-xiv LP) in the Student Text and quickly highlight the following:

- This is the second of three courses in <u>Exploring the Bible: The Dickinson Series</u>.

- Questions are the key to this study. Become an explorer/investigator.

- Pick your level of engagement—informal student or Extra Mile/certificate student.

- Keep a journal in which to record your personal reflections.

- During class time, we will only discuss a portion of what is in the Student Text. To get the full benefit of the material, you must do the homework.

Refer to the Covenant for Bible Study on page 200 (p. 270 LP) of the Student Text.

- Read the six principles aloud, with a different student reading each one.

- Ask whether everyone is comfortable with this covenant and willing to commit to it.

- See if there are questions or suggested additions.

- Ask: "Is there anything else we should practice to help make this a productive learning environment for all?"

- If not already mentioned by students, raise the question of the use of technology and social media during and after class sessions. For example:

Session 1 Activities

- *How will your group deal with cell phones?*
- *Are you open to having someone using Twitter to describe the class sessions to their followers?*
- *What about posting comments about class on social networking sites like Facebook?*
- *Write any suggestions on the newsprint/whiteboard and ask if students are willing to make these a part of their covenant.*

• If your group adds to the list, have students write the new items in the spaces provided on the Covenant page.

Bible Activity: Is It Soup Yet?
(30 Min)

Objective: To become familiar with the creation story in Genesis 1 and to examine that story in light of ancient notions of existence.

Part 1 *(10 min)*

- Ask students to turn to the section entitled Existence: It's Complicated on page 12 of the Student Text (p. 17 LP).

- Going around the room, have students take turns reading the paragraphs of that section through the examination of Genesis 1, ending with the paragraph on page 14 (p. 20 LP) that concludes "Each day of creation in Genesis 1 has those same three 'existence' elements."

Notes

Session 1 Activities

Notes

Existence: It's Complicated

One of the overarching themes of the stories in Genesis 1–11 is the theme of origins, and the creation stories kick us off with the origin of the earth itself.

One of the things that always baffled me about the story of creation in Genesis 1 was the conflict between what I was taught—that God created the universe out of nothing—and the words of the actual text. "Wait," I thought, "God's not starting from scratch. There's *stuff* there. There's this formless, voidy, primordial soup (Genesis 1:2). Well, where did *that* come from? Who made *that*?"

The reason I had that question was that I am a child of the modern age. To me, physical existence is about matter. If I can see it, touch it, and stub my toe on it, then it exists. I give some ground to make room for the existence of a spiritual realm, where the rules might be a bit different, but in the world of physical matter, to exist is to occupy space.

What I learned, however, was that the ancient Near East had a very different notion of what it meant to "exist." For them, the primordial soup that so troubled me did not exist, even if you could have drowned in it. For them, three criteria had to be met before anything could be said to "exist":

1. It must be separated out as a distinct entity;

2. It must be given a function;

3. It must be given a name.

Session 1 Activities

Existence: It's Complicated *Cont.*

Let's say I'm an ancient woodcarver staring at a big, long log. I begin to carve out the middle of it just to see what's in there. In a few days I'm looking at the world's first dugout canoe (the earliest one known is from Africa in 8000 B.C.E.). Have I created the canoe? Does it exist? Nope.

It doesn't exist because it has only met the first of the three criteria for existence. It has been separated out from the log as a distinct entity. But I still don't know what it's for and when I try to explain it to my kids I just call it "my log." The kids come down to see what I'm up to and all of a sudden there's a downpour. It rains so hard and so fast that the low-lying area around my log floods. The water is rising and the kids are scared, so I scoop them out of the knee-high water and put them in my log, getting in with them to calm their fears.

The rain continues and in short order my log, with us in it, actually begins to float. I'm fascinated and, clever soul that I am, I begin to see how I might get further out into the river to fish with my log. By golly, there's a purpose for this thing! Ding. Criteria number two is met. By now the kids have forgotten that it's pouring and are filled with the wonder of sitting inside a floating log. My daughter says, "Wow! This isn't a log. This is a cut-out-log-that-rides-on-water!" Bingo. There's a name, however crude, and my canoe now actually exists. Then my son leans too far to the right and we all very quickly learn to swim.

Notes

Session 1 Activities

Notes

Existence: It's Complicated *Cont.*

That three-fold understanding of existence—separation, function, and name—can be seen very clearly in the epic creation poem of Genesis 1. Let's look at it more closely:

> *In the beginning when God created the heavens and the earth, the earth was a formless void and darkness covered the face of the deep, while a wind from God swept over the face of the waters. (Genesis 1:1–2)*

By modern standards we have plenty of existing things in those first two verses. Apart from God, we have wind, we have water, and whatever else might be lurking under the "face of the deep." But the words "formless void" are key. To the ancients those words were the signal that nothing exists. Nothing has been differentiated from anything else.

> *Then God said, "Let there be light"; and there was light. And God saw that the light was good; and God separated the light from the darkness. God called the light Day, and the darkness he called Night. And there was evening and there was morning, the first day. (Genesis 1:3–5)*

Now we're talking. Or rather, God is talking. God doesn't just create photons here. God separates the light from the darkness that covered the deep we learned about back in verse 2. So now both light and dark are on their way to existence and, indeed, God continues that process by giving them names.

Notice those names, however. The names are not "light" and "dark." The names are "Day" and "Night." The names describe a function

Session 1 Activities

Existence: It's Complicated *Cont.*

and that function is further described in the phrase that echoes through each day of creation, "and there was evening and there was morning." God has not created matter here. God has created time, and as day follows day with the same refrain, God has created days and then put them together to form an entire week. Each day of creation in Genesis 1 has those same three "existence" elements.

Part II *(10 min)*

- Divide the class into groups of three to four.
- Give each group a copy of the handout, Is It Soup Yet?
- Ask them to fill in the handout by using what they've learned from the description of creation in Genesis 1.

Part III *(10 min)*

Bring the groups back together to discuss the following questions:

- Did anything surprise you in this exercise?
- Does seeing existence through the eyes of ancient cultures change how you see the creation stories? Life Connection Activity: Am I My Brother's Keeper? *(30 Min)*

Session 1 Activities

Notes

Life Connection Activity: Am I My Brother's Keeper?
(30 Min)

Objective: To become familiar with the story of Cain and Abel and to reflect on the message of that story for contemporary life and faith.

Part I *(7 min)*

- As a group, taking turns reading, read aloud the story of Cain and Abel in Genesis 4:1–16.
- Divide students into groups of two to three people.

Part II *(23 min)*

Ask each group to discuss the following questions (which should be written on the newsprint or on the board for easy reference).

- Why did Cain kill Abel?
- Can you think of contemporary examples of the same thing?
- Do you think there was a reason why God preferred one offering over the other? Does it matter?
- What is God's response to Cain's murder of Abel?
- What do you think of God's response?
- Is there a lesson here for siblings or others who might be rivals?
- What does the story tell us about the nature of God?
- What does the story tell us about the nature of human beings?

Session 1 Activities

REVIEW the homework for the next session on page 22 of the Student Text (p. 30 LP), making sure students understand the difference between the homework for informal and Extra Mile students. (5 min)

Homework (All Students)
The Old Testament is long and covers a period of several thousand years. Relative to that time frame, the reading doesn't take long at all. But this course has significantly more reading in between sessions than the first course did. Plan your time accordingly.

- ☐ Read through all of the Session 1 Student Text, including the Bible passage assignments in the clear boxes.

- ☐ Read through all of the Session 2 Student Text, including the Bible passage assignments in the clear boxes.

- ☐ Answer the questions in the Preparation for Check-in on page 48 (p. 66 LP).

Extra Mile (CEU and Certificate Students)
- ☐ Read the story of Jacob's reconciliation with Esau in Genesis 32:3–33:17.

- ☐ Read the parable of the Prodigal Son in Luke 15:11–32.

Notes

Session 1 Activities

Notes

- In an essay of five hundred to seven hundred words, reflect on the following questions:
  - What are the similarities in these stories?
  - What are the differences?
  - Do you think Jesus might have been thinking about Jacob and Esau when he told this parable?
  - What does each story teach about the nature of God and reconciliation?

Lesson Plan 2

WHO'S YOUR DADDY?

Objectives
- To examine two Old Testament stories that many find difficult and practice using some skills to deal with difficult texts.
- To begin to see the New Testament in light of its Jewish roots.
- To experience the relevance of ancient stories to contemporary life.

Materials Needed
- Nametags
- Bibles, newsprint and stand, whiteboard, or other means of posting information before students
- Markers (for the appropriate surface)
- Sheet with check-in questions
- Several study Bibles in different translations and with different perspectives
- Parking Lot list

Leader Preparation
- Read the student text for Session 2.
- Do the homework for this session listed at the end of Session 1, including the research for Extra Mile students.
- Determine whether you have any Extra Mile students and, if so, how many. Plan your time accordingly.
- Research any questions that came out of Session 1 for which you promised a response.
- Write out Check-in questions on newsprint or whiteboard. (You can save doing this each week if you write on something that can be saved and brought back to each session.)
- Become familiar with the texts and activities for the Session 2 class session.

Lesson Plan

- Become familiar with the appendix in the Student Text called, "Dealing with Difficult Texts" (p. 202 in Student Text, p. 272 LP) so that you can use these tools when needed throughout the course.

- Find and prepare needed materials.

- Write out the questions for Part II of the Bible Activity and post them so that small groups can easily look to them for reference.

- Write out the questions for Part II of the Life Connection Activity and post them so that small groups can easily look to them for reference.

Session 2 Activities

Check-In (10 Min)

From this session on, begin each class meeting with a ten-minute check-in. Each session should include the following (brief) responses from each person:

- What is one thing that was new to me in this material?
- What is one question that this week's topic raises for me?

This is not the time to discuss what they learned or to try to answer their questions. It's simply a way to note student observations and to spur the thinking of others.

Bible Activity: The Binding of Isaac (30 Min)

Objective: To make students familiar with one of the Bible's most famous stories and to give them some practice in dealing with texts that are problematic for many people.

Part I *(10 min)*

Invite students to recap the story, writing on the newsprint or board the various story elements as they are mentioned.

When the story recap is complete, make the following points about the story:

Notes

Session 2 Activities

Notes

- It is a very difficult story for many people. Remind students of Appendix 6, "Dealing with Difficult Texts" on page 202 of their Student Text (p. 272 LP) as a resource if they find this story troubling.

- It is a foundational story in the patriarchal narratives, designed to emphasize the incomparable faith of Abraham.

- It is mentioned in the New Testament in Hebrews 11:17–19.

- The story also appears in the Qur'an, but with some differences. The son in the Qur'an is not named, leading some Muslim scholars to believe it was Ishmael, not Isaac. In the Qur'an, the son is actually told of God's command and agrees to it.

- In the surrounding Canaanite culture of Abraham's time, child sacrifice was a common practice.

- The location of Mt. Moriah is disputed, but many believe it is the same location as the Temple Mount in Jerusalem.

Part II *(15 min)*

Divide the class into groups of two to three and ask each group to choose a reporter.

Once students are in their small groups, ask them to discuss the following questions (which should be written out where all can see for easy reference). Explain that students will only be reporting on the third question.

- What is your opinion of the story? Do you have issues with it? Why or why not?

- Read verses 7–8. Do you think Abraham was

Session 2 Activities

being dishonest with Isaac or did he really believe God would provide a way out?

- Read verses 15–18. Read Hebrews 11:17–19. What do these verses indicate about the purpose of this story?

Part III *(5 min)*

Bring the larger group back together and share responses to the third question.

Extra Mile Presentations *(13 Min)*

Extra Mile students were asked to compare and contrast the reconciliation of Jacob and Esau in Genesis 32–33 with the parable of the Prodigal Son in Luke 15:11–32. If you have Extra Mile students in your class, have them present jointly on their findings.

This comparison is a great set-up for the Life Application Activity that follows, so if you have no Extra Mile students, use this time to point out the similarities and differences yourself. It will help provide the larger context for Jacob's wrestling match. The following are some common threads between the two stories:

- Each involves a wealthy man with two sons.
- Each involves inheritance issues.
- Each has one son who has acted badly and another who has played by the rules.
- Each ends with a reconciliation.
- In each, the aggrieved party's forgiveness (Esau in Genesis and the father in the parable) is identified with the nature of God.

Notes

LESSON PLAN 2: WHO'S YOUR DADDY? 17

Session 2 Activities

Notes

Life Application Activity: The Wrestling Match (30 Min)

Objective: To allow students to become more familiar with a key story in the patriarchal period and to think about the way that story may connect to contemporary experiences of struggle.

Part I (5 min)

As before, recap the story of Jacob wrestling with the angel at the Jabbok River in Genesis 32:22–32, inviting students to volunteer elements of the story as you or a student record responses on the newsprint or board.

Divide the class into groups of two to three, aiming for different groupings than in the first exercise.

Part II (25 min)

Ask each group to discuss the following:

- Who is Jacob wrestling?
- In verse 28, Jacob's opponent seems to be saying that Jacob won the match. Did he? Does Jacob think he won?
- How is Jacob changed as a result?
- Why do you think this story is included in the Bible?
- Do you like this story? Why or why not?
- Do you think wrestling with God is ever an apt metaphor?
- Have you ever experienced situations when you felt like you were wrestling with God in some way?

Session 2 Activities

- Did those times change you in any way?
- Have you ever technically won some kind of challenge but felt somehow that you lost—or vice versa?

REVIEW of homework on page 48 of the Student Text (p. 67 LP). (5 min)

Homework (All Students)

☐ Read through all of the Session 3 Student Text, including the Bible passage assignments in the clear boxes.

☐ Think about the reflection questions in the text.

☐ Answer the questions in the Preparation for Check-in on page 48 (p. 66 LP).

Extra Mile (CEU and Certificate Students)

☐ Leviticus 25 describes laws by which debts were forgiven, slaves freed, and land returned to ancestral owners every fifty years. This became known as the Year of Jubilee. Research the practice of Jubilee in both ancient and modern times and write a report of approximately five hundred words describing your findings.

☐ Be prepared to share your findings briefly with the group during the next class session.

Notes

Lesson Plan

LAYING DOWN THE LAW 3

Objectives
- To recognize the role of women in some Old Testament texts.
- To examine the Ten Commandments in light of contemporary morality.
- To learn about the ancient practice of Jubilee and its contemporary significance.

Materials Needed
- Nametags
- Bibles, newsprint and stand, whiteboard, or other means of posting information before students
- Markers (for the appropriate surface)
- Sheet with check-in questions
- Several study Bibles in different translations and with different perspectives
- Parking Lot list
- Your own research on the Jubilee

Handouts
- The Ten Commandments (pages 65-66)

Leader Preparation
- Read the student text for Session 3.
- Do the homework at the end of Session 2, including the Extra Mile research.
- Become familiar with the texts and activities for the Session 3 class session.
- Determine whether you or Extra Mile students will present the information on the Jubilee.
- Write out and post the passages in Part I of the Bible Activity for easy reference.
- Write out and post the passages in Part I of the Life Connection Activity for easy reference.
- Find and prepare needed materials and handouts.
- Research any questions in the Parking Lot for which you promised a response.

Session 3 Activities

Notes

Check-In (10 Min)

Ask each student to respond to the following two questions about the Session 3 material they read for homework:

- What is one thing that was new to me in this material?
- What is one question that this week's topic raises for me?

Bible Activity: Women Heroes (30 Min)

Objective: *To become familiar with three stories from this period in which women played significant roles.*

Part I *(15 min)*

Divide the class evenly into three groups.

Assign a different one of the following passages to each group:

- Exodus 1:8–2:10
- Joshua 2:1–24, Joshua 6:22–25
- Judges 4:1–24

Ask students to read the passage aloud in their groups and then respond to the following questions (which should be written out on the board or on newsprint for easy reference):

- What were the names of the women mentioned in your passage?
- Who were they?

Session 3 Activities

- What is the overall story told in your passage and how did each woman contribute?

Make sure each group is aware that they will be reporting their responses back to the full class.

Part II *(15 min)*

Ask each group to share the answers to the three questions with the full class so that everyone hears all three stories. Allow five minutes for each group to present.

Extra Mile Presentations (15 Min)

Extra Mile students were asked to research the practice of Jubilee in both ancient and contemporary times. Now that the class as a whole is familiar with the original passage, allow any Extra Mile students to present their findings.

If you do not have Extra Mile students, you should present this information. You can find articles about the practice by searching the word "Jubilee" on Wikipedia. Reading the articles on Jubilee (biblical) and Jubilee (Christianity) should give you enough information.

Life Connection Activity: The Ten Commandments (30 Min)

Objective: To help students become aware that there are two listings of the Ten Commandments with a slight variation and to allow them to probe possible meanings of individual commandments more deeply.

Session 3 Activities

Notes

Part I (10 min)

Ask for two volunteers to read the Sabbath commandment, noting for the group that it is the longest commandment of the ten. Have one student read from the listing in Exodus 20:8–11 and the other from Deuteronomy 5:12–15.

Ask the group to identify the difference between the two presentations. (The Exodus rendering grounds the motivation for the Sabbath command in the creation story, while the Deuteronomy version lists Israel's experience with slavery as the reason.)

Reflect with the group on the following questions:

- Why do you think the commandment differs in that way?
- Does the alternate motivation make a difference in the meaning of the commandment?

Part II (15 min)

- Distribute the handout The Ten Commandments, and divide the class into groups of three to four.
- Explain that while the wording of the commandments is quite simple, there are lots of questions that can be raised about their meaning.
- Ask each group to select two of the commandments and write an explanation of their meaning for an inquiring teenager.
- Encourage at least one member of each group to think like a teen and ask questions about the meaning.

Session 3 Activities

- Remind groups that the text (in Exodus 20:1–17) gives some additional meaning beyond what is written on the handout.

Part III *(5 min)*

- Allow groups to share their explanations with one another.

REVIEW of homework for Session 4 on page 71 of the Student Text (p. 101 LP). (5 min)

Homework (All Students)

☐ Read the Student Text for Session 4 along with the associated Bible readings. **Plan ahead, as Session 4 has more reading than previous sessions.**

☐ Think about the reflection questions in the text.

☐ Review the assignment for the Extra Mile students. Find and listen to one musical setting of a psalm.

Notes

Session 3 Activities

Notes

Extra Mile (CEU and Certificate Students)

Every single psalm has been put to music multiple times and some are quite famous. From classical works to rap, there are renditions of psalms in almost every musical genre.

- ☐ Find musical settings (in any style) for three different psalms to share with the class. Work with your group facilitator on how best to present what you find.

- ☐ Possible types of sharing could include:
  - Having the group sing the hymns/songs. Many are printed in denominational hymnals and songbooks.
  - Ask a musician in your group to play and/or sing them.
  - Play a music track.
  - Find a video performance of the music on YouTube and share that.
  - Invite a musician from your community to join you for this segment of the class and perform.

Note that if there are several Extra Mile students in your class, you may not have time to share all three, so you should pick a favorite song in case there is only time for one of the selections you have chosen.

Lesson Plan

UNITED WE STAND

4

Objectives

- To examine two famous passages of the Bible.
- To hear and experience the Bible as music.
- To examine the practice of repentance and confession.

Materials Needed

- Nametags
- Bibles, newsprint and stand, whiteboard, or other means of posting information before students
- Markers (for the appropriate surface)
- Sheet with check-in questions
- Several study Bibles in different translations and with different perspectives
- Parking Lot list
- Method for sharing the music in the Extra Mile presentation. See the note for the Extra Mile presentation on page 26.
- Your own musical selections

Leader Preparation

- Read the student text for Session 4
- Do the homework listed at the end of Session 3, including the Extra Mile research. (You can find music suggestions on p. 59 of this guide.)
- Become familiar with the texts and activities for the Session 4 class session.
- Determine how you will present and use music in this session. Plan the technology accordingly.
- Invite any guest musicians to your class, if you choose to use them.
- Make sure your use of music will not disturb those who are not part of your group but might be near to your class setting.
- Write out and post the signs of repentance listed in Part II of the Bible Activity for easy reference.
- Write out and post the reflection questions listed in Part II of the Bible Activity for easy reference.

Lesson Plan

- Write out and post the discussion questions listed in Part II of the Life Connection Activity for easy reference.

- Research any Parking Lot questions for which you promised a response.

- Find and prepare needed materials and handouts.

- **Prepare a list for the Massachusetts Bible Society of all students who you anticipate will complete the course as Extra Mile students, making sure all names are spelled correctly.**

- Send the list of names to dsadmin@massbible.org and indicate the postal address where certificates should be sent.

- Note that the Certificate of Participation you will give to informal students is available for you to download and print yourself at exploringthebible.org/forms. You only need to request the Certificate of Completion for Extra Mile students from MBS.

Session 4 Activities

Check-In (10 Min)

Ask each student to respond to the following two questions about the Session 3 material they read for homework:

- What is one thing that was new to me in this material?
- What is one question that this week's topic raises for me?

This is not the time to discuss what students have learned or to try to answer their questions. It's simply a way to note student observations and to spur the thinking of others.

Bible Activity: Repent (30 Min)

Objectives: *To learn about the context and message of Psalm 51 and to examine the nature of repentance in light of that knowledge.*

Part 1 *(7 min)* *Ask students to turn to Psalm 51.* Bring to their attention:

- The first seventy-two psalms are attributed to King David.
- Some of the psalms of David are tied to specific events in his life.
- Psalm 51 represents David's prayer after the prophet Nathan confronts him about David's sin with Bathsheba. (Point out that this circumstance is noted at the beginning of the psalm.)

Notes

Session 4 Activities

Notes

- Verses 18–19 are probably a later addition. In David's time, the walls of Jerusalem were standing strong and did not need rebuilding. These verses were likely added during the Exile, after the destruction of Jerusalem, to adapt the psalm for liturgical use.

Going around the room, having students take turns, read the psalm aloud. (Parts of this psalm have been made into hymns and songs. If you have a group with musical talents, feel free to incorporate the music in some way.)

Part II *(23 min)*

Divide the class into two groups. Ask each group to find the following signs of repentance in the psalm:

- Acknowledgment of sin
- Expressions of regret
- Request for forgiveness
- Acceptance of consequences

When they have identified those four elements, ask them to discuss the following questions (which should be written out on the newsprint or board):

- Remembering that David impregnated the wife of one of his most trusted soldiers (Uriah) and then arranged for Uriah's death to cover it up, do you find this an acceptable show of repentance? Why or why not?
- What does David's request for forgiveness tell us about David's character?
- What does it tell us about God's character?

Session 4 Activities

Extra Mile Presentations (15 Min)

Note: If you have a lot of songs here, you could listen to/sing a few and use the rest in other ways. For example, you might open or close future sessions with some of them, or invite those who wish to remain after the close of the formal class session to listen to the rest of the music. You might also think of other ways this music might be shared.

- Extra Mile students were asked to find three psalms that became hymns or praise songs and to find a way to share the music for at least one of them with the class.

- Remind students that the Psalms were (and are) Israel's songbook. They were not poems and prayers to be read but songs to be sung in liturgical settings.

- Ask the Extra Mile students to share these hymns/songs during this time in whatever way is most appropriate for your group. (You will probably have time for about three songs.) Possible types of sharing could include:
  - *Having the group sing the hymns/songs. Many are printed in denominational hymnals and songbooks.*
  - *Ask a musician in your group to play and/or sing them.*
  - *Play a music track.*
  - *Find a video performance of the music on YouTube and share that.*

Notes

Session 4 Activities

Notes

If you have no Extra Mile students, select several musical settings from the Psalms yourself and share them with the class. A list of suggestions can be found on page 67 of this guide.

Life Connection Activity: Seasons (30 Min)

Objectives: *To become familiar with a famous portion of the Bible, to expand that knowledge by examining the full context, and to listen for resonance or discord with a student's own life and beliefs.*

Part I *(10 min)*

Taking turns around the room, read Ecclesiastes 3:1–8 aloud. Or, instead of reading these verses, you could also play one of the many recordings of these verses in song. "Turn! Turn! Turn!" is just one memorable example.

Discuss the following:

- How many of you have heard this passage before? Where?
- Did you know it was from the Bible?
- Is it a passage you can relate to?

Part II *(20 min)*

- Divide the class into groups of two to three.
- Ask students to read the rest of Ecclesiastes 3 aloud in their small groups and discuss the following questions (which should be written out on the newsprint or board):

Session 4 Activities

- *What do you think is the writer's mood in these verses? Why?*
- *What do these verses say about heaven and the afterlife?*
- *Is there anything in these verses that you find troubling?*
- *Is there anything in these verses that you find comforting?*

REVIEW of homework for Session 5 on page 107 of the Student Text (p. 146 LP). (5 min)

Homework (All Students)

☐ Read the Student Text for Session 5 along with the associated Bible readings.

☐ Think about the reflection questions in the text.

Extra Mile (CEU and Certificate Students)

☐ Choose one of the "Minor Prophets" from the period covered in
Session 5:
Hosea   Obadiah   Habakkuk   Joel
Micah   Zephaniah Amos   Nahum

☐ Research the prophet you have chosen—both the man and his writing—and prepare a report of about five hundred words on what you have found.

Be prepared to share the major points in the next class session.

Notes

Lesson Plan

DIVIDED WE FALL

5

Objectives
- To become familiar with several famous stories from the prophets.
- To better understand the role of the ancient prophet.
- To see the prophets in light of our common humanity.

Materials Needed
- Nametags
- Bibles, newsprint and stand, whiteboard, or other means of posting information before students
- Markers (for the appropriate surface)
- Sheet with check-in questions
- Several study Bibles in different translations and with different perspectives
- Parking Lot list
- Your own research on the Minor Prophets

Leader Preparation
- Read the Student Text for Session 5.
- Do the homework found at the end of Session 4, including the Extra Mile research.
- Become familiar with the texts and activities for the Session 5 class session.
- Write out and post the passages in Part I of the Bible Activity for easy reference.
- Write out and post the questions in Part II of the Bible Activity for easy reference.
- Write out and post the questions in Part II of the Life Activity for easy reference.
- Research any Parking Lot questions for which you promised a response.
- Find and prepare needed materials.
- **If you have not yet sent the list of names for Extra Mile certificates to dsdmin@massbible.org, do so immediately or you will not have certificates for the final session.**

Session 5 Activities

Notes

Check-In (10 Min)

Ask each student to respond to the following two questions about the Session 4 material they read for homework:

- What is one thing that was new to me in this material?
- What is one question that this week's topic raises for me?

This is not the time to discuss what students have learned or to try to answer their questions. It's simply a way to note student observations and to spur the thinking of others.

Bible Activity: Object Lessons (30 Min)

Objectives: *To explore some well-known object lessons from the Major Prophets to become more familiar with the texts and with the role of the prophet.*

Part I *(10 min)*

Divide the class into four groups and assign each group a different one of the following passages:

- Isaiah 20:1–6
- Jeremiah 19:1–15
- Jeremiah 32:1–15
- Ezekiel 4:1–17

Ask each group to record their answers to the following questions (which should be written on the newsprint or on the board for easy reference).

Session 5 Activities

- What, exactly, did God ask the prophet to do?
- Was it done publicly or privately?
- Who was the audience?
- What did the act symbolize?

Part II *(20 min)*

Ask the groups to come back together and have each group share the information about their passage.

Lead a discussion of the following questions:

- What purpose do you think these object lessons served? Why not just speak the message?
- Do you think these sorts of object lessons would have been effective? Why or why not?
- Are there contemporary examples of this kind of thing, where there is a symbolic physical display of a message of either warning or hope?
- This can turn to a general discussion of the use of symbols in our culture. There are hateful warnings like the use of a swastika or burning cross. There are loving hopes expressed in makeshift memorials at the site of a tragedy. There are planned, official expressions of hope or mourning in Holocaust museums, war memorials, or monuments to important individuals. What role do these play in our lives?
- Do you find such object lessons helpful?

Notes

Session 5 Activities

Notes

Extra Mile Presentations (15 Min)

Extra Mile students were asked to choose one of the Minor Prophets from this period and research information about the prophet and his writing. Ask those students to share their findings.

If there are no Extra Mile students, you may want to review the section on the prophets from the first course. The section can be found at the back of the Student Text beginning on page 184 (p. 254 LP).

Life Connection Activity (30 Min)

Objectives: *To become familiar with a famous story about Elijah and to think about whether that story might resonate with someone in difficult circumstances today.*

Part I *(10 min)*

Taking turns around the group, read aloud 1 Kings 19:1–21. Ask the group to identify the following:

- The use of a symbolic number. (Answer: forty—in verse 8)

- The name of a famous song. (Answer: "Sounds of Silence"—in verse 12. Clearest in the NRSV translation.)

38 INTRODUCING THE OLD TESTAMENT

Session 5 Activities

Part II *(20 min)*

Divide the class into groups of two to three.

Ask each group to discuss the following questions (have them written out in front of the class for easy reference):

- Why is Elijah so dejected?
- What does he do about it?
- How does God respond?
- Look at how God appears in verses 11–13. Is there anything in those verses you relate to? What do they teach about the God of Israel?
- Have you ever felt like Elijah under the broom tree?
- Does this passage seem comforting or disconcerting for someone in Elijah's circumstances?
- Does anything in this passage resonate with you?
- Does anything in this passage trouble you?

REVIEW of homework for Session 6 from Student Text. (5 min)

Notes

Session 5 Activities

Notes

Homework (All Students)

- ☐ Read the student text for Session 6, including all Bible reading.

- ☐ Think about the reflection questions.

- ☐ You've read a lot of stories throughout the Old Testament. You've also seen some major thematic arcs: covenant, exile and return, captivity and freedom, sin and repentance. Select either a particular story or a broad theme that stood out for you and plan to share your selection with the group at the final class session. You will be asked to share in the following ways:

  - Identify the story or theme, including (for particular stories) the chapter and verses in the Bible where it can be found.

  - Was this a story/theme that was familiar to you before the course or was it new to you?

  - Why did this particular story/theme stand out for you? Was it just a good story? Did it either connect with or challenge something you had believed or experienced in your own life? Did it generate new understanding in some way?

  - Is it a story you would tell your children or grandchildren or do you think it is best kept for adult discussion?

Extra Mile (CEU and Certificate Students)

- ☐ In five hundred to seven hundred words, write out your response to the last set of questions in the homework for all students.

Lesson Plan

AGE OF EMPIRES

6

Objectives

- To look back on the experience of this exposure to the Old Testament and reflect.
- To make a personal connection to an ancient text.
- To identify questions or issues that need follow-up.
- To celebrate the achievements of the students in completing the course.

Materials Needed

- Nametags
- Bibles, newsprint and stand, whiteboard, or other means of posting information before students
- Markers (for the appropriate surface)
- Sheet with check-in questions
- Several study Bibles in different translations and with different perspectives
- Parking Lot list
- Student certificates
  - Certificates of Participation for Informal Students. Download these from exploringthebible.org/forms and fill them out yourself. Be sure to pick the certificate from course 2.
  - Certificates of Completion for any Extra Mile and CEU students. These are prepared and sent by the Massachusetts Bible Society. **If you did not request them ahead of time (as instructed in Sesions 4 and 5), you can still request them but may have to get them to your student at a later date.**
- Other items for your celebration—for example, a meal, cake, or other refreshments; other tokens of accomplishment that are unique to your group

LESSON PLAN 6: AGE OF EMPIRES 41

Lesson Plan

Handouts
- Student Evaluation (p. 47) with #10 blank envelopes. You will need one set for each student.

Leader Preparation
- Read Session 6 in the Student Text.
- Do the homework listed at the end of Session 5.
- Become familiar with the core activity of the Session 6 class session. Be prepared to share your own story if group members are reluctant to begin.
- Write and post the items to share (under the third bullet point of Telling Stories) for easy reference.
- Write and post the wrap-up questions for easy reference.
- **Become familiar with the completion activities that follow this session** to make sure your students get proper credit and can be made aware of future opportunities.
- Find and prepare needed materials.

Session 6 Activities

Check-In (10 Min)

Ask each student to respond to the following two questions about the Session 6 material they read for homework:

- What is one thing that was new to me in this material?
- What is one question that this week's topic raises for me?

This is not the time to discuss what students have learned or to try to answer their questions. It's simply a way to note student observations and to spur the thinking of others.

Telling Stories (60 Min)

Objectives: To help students become aware of the grounding of the biblical narratives in particular places and times and the way that grounding is connected to historical research.

The bulk of this class session consists of students sharing their choice of an Old Testament story or theme that stood out for them, as they were asked to reflect on in the homework.

If you have a particularly large class, consider dividing the class in half and selecting a person in each group to facilitate the sharing process. If you will have more than one group, the sharing guide that follows should be written out ahead of time and placed where all can see.

Notes

Session 6 Activities

Notes

Being sensitive to those who might find sharing more difficult, encourage students to talk about the story/theme they have selected in the following ways:

- Identify the story or theme, including (for particular stories) the chapter and verses in the Bible where it can be found.

- Was this a story/theme that was familiar to you before the course or was it new to you?

- Why did this particular story/theme stand out for you? Was it just a good story? Did it either connect with or challenge something you had believed or experienced in your own life? Did it generate new understanding in some way?

- Is it a story you would tell your children or grandchildren or do you think it is best kept for adult discussion?

Wrap-Up (10 Min)

- Remind students of the "Help! I Have Questions!" section on page 201 in their Student Text (p. 271 LP) (Appendix 5) to resolve any questions that remain unanswered for them from the course material or to help with new questions that may arise from continued study.

This is a time to get oral feedback about the full course. The written evaluation is done in the next section (page 47).

- Appoint someone (maybe yourself) to take detailed notes about the responses to better inform your facilitator's evaluation.

Session 6 Activities

- Ask the following questions:
    - *What were your expectations for this course and were those expectations met?*
    - *Did you enjoy the class activities? What was appealing about them? What wasn't appealing?*
    - *Do you like the Old Testament more (or less) now than when you started? How did this class contribute to this?*
    - *Did this course make you more (or less) interested in delving more deeply into the Old Testament?*
    - *Was there anything you learned about the Old Testament that really surprised you?*
    - *Did you feel that the course was unbiased in its approach to the text?*
    - *Is there additional feedback you would like to provide to the Massachusetts Bible Society?*

Evaluation and Celebration
(10 Min)

- Collect any outstanding homework from Extra Mile students and remind them of the last homework assignment for this lesson on page 176 of the Student Text (p. 241 LP).

- Congratulate all students and hand out their certificates one by one. Recognize the hard work they have put into the course and sing their praises. Celebrate the accomplishment of your students!

Notes

Session 6 Activities

Notes

- Hand out the student evaluations and envelopes. Students should fill out the evaluations **at this session** and seal them in the envelope before turning them back in to you.

- Before letting students go, remind them that this is just the second of three, six-week courses in <u>Exploring the Bible: The Dickinson Series</u>. They can continue to learn with this series or with many other available Bible studies and materials.

Once the Final Session Is Complete

Mail the following back to the Massachusetts Bible Society:

- Student Evaluations
- Your Facilitator Evaluation
- Homework from your Extra Mile students
- Your notes about the performance of the Extra Mile students
- Your class contact list (See the note in the Gathering section of Session 1 on p. 2 for the assurances of how this list is and is not used.)

Please return this evaluation to:
Massachusetts Bible Society, 199 Herrick Rd.,
Newton Centre, MA 02459
or e-mail to dsadmin@massbible.org.

STUDENT EVALUATION

! **Course (circle one):**   I   II   III

Why did you take this course? Were your expectations met?

Did you do this study with a group or on your own?   ☐ Group   ☐ Alone

! Did you take this course for certification or CEUs?   ☐ Yes   ☐ No
If yes, please be sure that all of your written work is submitted to the Massachusetts Bible Society by either yourself or your group leader at the conclusion of the course.

Did your group have a mix of "Extra Mile" and informal students?   ☐ Yes   ☐ No

     If "yes," did you find the mix helpful?   ☐ Yes   ☐ No

     Why or why not?

STUDENT EVALUATION

Who was your group leader? _____

Scale: 1 - most negative, 10 - most positive

Please rate your leader on the following using a scale of 1-10.

_____ Creating a welcoming and inclusive environment

_____ Keeping the class sessions on track

_____ Beginning and ending on time

_____ Handling conflicting opinions with respect

_____ Being prepared for class sessions

Scale: 1 - most negative, 10 - most positive

Please rate the physical setting for your group on the following using a scale of 1-10.

_____ The space was free of distractions and interruptions

_____ The space was physically comfortable and conductive to learning

_____ The group could easily adjust to different configurations

_____ It was easy to see instructional materials and group members

_____ Restroom facilities were easily accessible

_____ The space was accessible to those with disabilities

Do you have a particular faith tradition or spiritual orientation? If so, how would you name it?

_____

Did you feel that your opinions and perspective were respected in the following areas:

Course materials?   ☐ Yes   ☐ No

Class discussions?   ☐ Yes   ☐ No

By the group leader?   ☐ Yes   ☐ No

STUDENT EVALUATION

If you were an "informal student" (i.e., not a student seeking certification or CEUs), how much of the homework and reading did you complete? Please describe on a scale of 1-10, with 1 being virtually none and 10 being all of it.

_____

Did you do any of the Extra Mile assignments? ☐ Yes ☐ No

Scale: 1 - most negative, 10 - most positive

Please rate the quality of the homework assignments using a scale of 1-10.

_____ It was easy to understand the assignment

_____ The work could reasonably be completed between sessions

_____ I learned important things from doing the homework

_____ I did not feel pushed to come to a particular conclusion

Please answer the following questions:

Did you visit the Exploring the Bible Facebook page or follow us on Twitter @ExploreBible? Do you find these tools useful in staying connected to the Exploring the Bible community? Are there other ways you would prefer to be connected? If you would like to be on the Exploring the Bible e-mail list, please include your e-mail address in the space below.

Did this study answer any questions you had at the beginning? What were some of the most important questions that were answered for you?

STUDENT EVALUATION

Did anything disappoint you in this study? Was there something you expected that was not provided? Questions you really wanted answered that were not?

What new questions do you have upon completion that you did not have at the beginning? Do you find those new questions exciting or frustrating?

Did you learn anything of interest to you from this study? If you studied with a group, indicate how much of that came from the material provided and how much from the group discussion.

Have your impressions/beliefs/thoughts about the Bible changed as a result of this study? In what way?

STUDENT EVALUATION

Would you recommend this study to a friend?

How would you rate this study using a scale of 1-10, with 1 being not at all helpful and 10 being exceptionally helpful.

Other thoughts, comments, or suggestions?

Please return this evaluation to:
Massachusetts Bible Society, 199 Herrick Rd.,
Newton Centre, MA 02459
or e-mail to dsadmin@massbible.org.

Please return this evaluation to:
Massachusetts Bible Society, 199 Herrick Rd.,
Newton Centre, MA 02459
or e-mail to dsadmin@massbible.org.

FACILITATOR EVALUATION

Your Name: _____

Date the course began: _____

Date the course was completed: _____

Meeting location: _____

Course (circle one):   I   II   III

Respond to the following questions about the demographics of your group:

How many were in the group at the beginning?

How many were typically in attendance at any given session?

What ages were represented in your group?

Did any drop out? If so, did they give a reason?

What was the gender representation in your group?

Describe the racial/ethnic representation in your group:

Did you have group members who self-identified as being of no particular faith tradition other than Christian?

How many in your group were Extra Mile students?

Please comment about your class dynamics:

Did you feel adequately prepared to lead this group? Is there anything this guide or more training could have supplied to make the experience easier?

Scale: 1 - most negative, 10 - most positive

Please rate the Leader's Guide on the following using a scale of 1-10.

_____ The Leader's Guide was easy to understand and follow

_____ The class activities were appropriate to the session topic

_____ The class activities engaged the students in a positive way

_____ The class activities could be completed within the time allotted

_____ I always knew what to do in preparation for the next session

_____ I could fit preparation for sessions into my schedule easily

_____ The class flowed smoothly from beginning to end

_____ I was pleased with the overall quality of the Leader's Guide

Please respond to the following questions:

Did you encounter anything in class sessions that you felt unprepared to handle? If so, what?

To what extent did the students in your group know one another at the beginning of the course?

Did the group gain cohesion over the six sessions?

To what extent did the students do the homework and reading?

Did you personally enjoy facilitating this group? Why or why not? Would you do it again?

Other thoughts, comments, or suggestions?

Please return this evaluation to:
*Massachusetts Bible Society, 199 Herrick Rd.,
Newton Centre, MA 02459
or e-mail to dsadmin@massbible.org.*

Massachusetts Bible Society Statement on Scripture

The Massachusetts Bible Society is an ecumenical, Christian organization with a broad diversity of Scriptural approaches and interpretations among its members and supporters. The following statement on the nature of Scripture represents the guiding principle for our selection of programming and resources, but agreement with it is neither a pre-requisite for membership nor a litmus test for grant recipients.

> The Bible was written by many authors, all inspired by God. It is neither a simple collection of books written by human authors, nor is it the literal words of God dictated to human scribes. It is a source of religious truth, presented in a diversity of styles, genres, and languages and is not meant to serve as fact in science, history, or social structure.
>
> The Bible has authority for communities of faith who take time to study and prayerfully interpret its message, but it is also important for anyone who wants more fully to understand culture, religious thought, and the world in which we live.
>
> Biblical texts have been interpreted in diverse ways from generation to generation and are always filtered through the lens of the reader's faith and life experiences. This breadth and plurality, however, are what keep the Bible alive through the ages and enhance its ongoing, transformative power.

A Covenant for Bible Study

We covenant together to deal with our differences in a spirit of mutual respect and to refrain from actions that may harm the emotional and physical well-being of others.

The following principles will guide our actions:

- **We will treat others whose views may differ from our own with the same courtesy we would want to receive ourselves.**
- **We will listen with a sincere desire to understand the point of view being expressed by another person, especially if it is different from our own.**
- **We will respect each other's ideas, feelings, and experiences.**
- **We will refrain from blaming or judging in our attitude and behavior towards others.**
- **We will communicate directly with any person with whom we may disagree in a respectful and constructive way.**
- **We will seek feedback to ensure that we have truly understood each other in our communications.**

Additional agreements for our particular group:

Class Contact

Your Name: _____

Date the course began: _____

Date the course was completed: _____

Meeting location: _____

Please provide your preferred phone number and e-mail address.

Name	Phone	E-mail

Name Me, Please

In Genesis 2:19, God brings all the animals to Adam so that Adam might give them a name. But there were three that stumped him. Can you help Adam out by inventing a name for these three creatures?

_____

_____

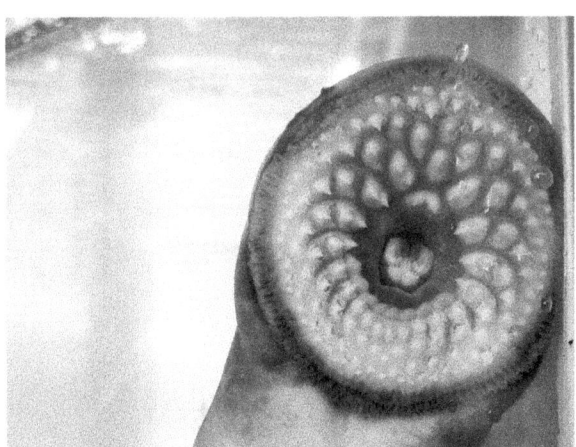

_____

Is it Soup Yet?

In the ancient Near East, three criteria had to be fulfilled in order to say something existed:
1. It must be separated out as a *distinct entity*;
2. It must be given a *function*;
3. It must be given a *name*.

Turn in your Bible to Genesis 1. For each day of creation, make note of each of the three steps.		
What is separated?	What is its function?	What is its name?
DAY 1		
DAY 2		
DAY 3		
DAY 4		
DAY 5		
DAY 6		

The Ten Commandments

Put the following commandments into your own words, as if you were explaining their meaning to a teenager. One of your group members should take the role of the teen, asking questions about the meaning to help the group explore the depth of the commandment.

Wording is taken from Exodus 20:1–17 in the New Revised Standard Version of the Bible and includes only the main line of the commandment as it is usually listed. Refer to the text for additional elaboration.

> **Note:** Jews, Catholics, and Protestants all number the Ten Commandments differently. Since the listing most frequently seen in American culture is the Protestant version, that is the one adopted for the purposes of this handout.

1. You shall have no other gods before me.

2. You shall not make for yourself an idol.

3. You shall not make wrongful use of the name of the LORD your God.

4. Remember the Sabbath day, and keep it holy.

5. Honor your father and your mother.

6. You shall not murder.

7. You shall not commit adultery.

8. You shall not steal.

9. You shall not bear false witness against your neighbor.

10. You shall not covet.

A Sampling of Music Resources for Session 4

Hymns

"A Mighty Fortress" PSALM 46
"From All That Dwell Below the Skies" PSALM 117
"Hail to the Lord's Anointed" PSALM 72
"Joyful, Joyful We Adore Thee" PSALM 71
"Lift Up Your Heads, Ye Mighty Gates" PSALM 24
"Lord, Thou Hast Searched Me and Dost Know" PSALM 139
"O God Our Help In Ages Past" PSALM 90
"O Worship the King" PSALM 104
"Praise My Soul the King of Heaven" PSALM 103
"Praise To the Lord, The Almighty" PSALMS 103 & 105

Other

"40" U2 PSALM 40
"Brother James Air" PSALM 23
"By the Rivers of Babylon" The Melodians PSALM 137
"By the Waters of Babylon" Sweet Honey in the Rock PSALM 137
"House of God, Forever" Jon Foreman PSALM 23
John Michael Talbott:
    "Psalm 51"
    "Psalm 62"
    "Psalm 151"
"On the Willows" from *Godspell* PSALM 137
"Psalm 23" Sin Dizzy
"Psalm 40:2" The Mountain Goats
"Psalm 51" Charlie Peacock
"Shepherd Psalm" John Carter PSALM 23
"The 23rd Psalm" Bobby McFerrin

Classical

Chichester Psalms Leonard Bernstein

"I Will Lift Up Mine Eyes" John Rutter **PSALM 121**

"Laudate Dominum" Mozart **PSALM 117**

Messiah Handel (by movement number):

    27–28 **PSALM 22**

    29 **PSALM 69**

    32 **PSALM 16**

    33 **PSALM 24**

    36–37 **PSALM 68**

    40–43 **PSALM 2**

Requiem Johannes Brahms:

    "Wie Lieblich Sind Deine Wohnungen" **PSALM 84**

    "Herr, Lehre Dich Mich" **PSALM 39**

    "Selig Sind" **PSALM 126**

"Simple Song" Leonard Bernstein **PSALM 121**

Symphony of Psalms Igor Stravinsky

The Creation Haydn:

    "The Heavens Are Telling" **PSALM 19**

"The Lord Is My Shepherd" John Rutter **PSALM 23**

Praise Songs

"As the Deer" **PSALM 42**

"Bless His Holy Name" **PSALM 103**

"Glorify Thy Name" **PSALM 86**

"I Will Call Upon the Lord" **PSALM 18**

"O, Lord, Hear My Prayer" **PSALM 86**

"Praise the Lord With the Sound of Trumpet" **PSALM 150**

"Thy Word Is a Lamp" **PSALM 119**

Sample Advertising Blurbs for Introducing the Old Testament

> Longer bulletin inserts, brochures, and/or posters can be supplied on request.

For Christian Audiences

How often have you thought, "I don't even know enough about the Bible to attend a Bible study—I'd be completely lost." Exploring the Bible: The Dickinson Series is a set of small-group studies made exactly for you. Introducing the Old Testament is the second course in this series and will help you become familiar with both this ancient set of writings and the historical context surrounding them. Come with us back to the Early Stone Age and learn what they never taught you in Sunday School.

The second six-week course in this series, Introducing the Old Testament, will be offered [**provide your information here**]. Contact [**provide local contact**] to express your interest. The class can be taken either informally or to receive Continuing Education Units and/or eventual certification in biblical literacy.

To find out more please visit exploringthebible.org/faq.

For Mixed Audiences

Adam and Eve, Noah, Joseph and that dreamcoat of his; from classical art to modern politics to Hollywood and Broadway, this ancient collection of texts and its characters are woven into the fabric of western civilization.

Exploring the Bible: The Dickinson Series is a series of three, six-week courses about the Bible and its contents. Designed to teach, not preach, these courses focus on the Christian Bible and the stories that have shaped so much of the culture in which we live.

The second six-week study, Introducing the Old Testament, is being offered [**provide local information**]. Contact [**provide local contact**] to express your interest. The class can be taken either informally or to receive Continuing Education Units and/or eventual certification in biblical literacy.

To find out more please visit exploringthebible.org/faq.

Glossary from Student Text

A.D.
Abbreviation for the Latin Anno Domini, meaning "in the year of the Lord." A system of notating time, generally used with B.C.

Antichrist
With a small "a" it is one who denies or opposes Christ. With a capital "A" it refers to a great antagonist expected to fill the world with wickedness but to be conquered forever by Christ at his second coming.

Apocalypse (adj. apocalyptic)
One of the Jewish and Christian writings of 200 B.C.E. to 150 C.E. marked by pseudonymity, symbolic imagery, and the expectation of an imminent cosmic cataclysm in which God destroys the ruling powers of evil and raises the righteous to life in a messianic kingdom.

Apocrypha
Books included in the Septuagint and Vulgate but excluded from the Jewish and Protestant canons of the Old Testament.

Ark
Something that affords protection and safety. Two different forms of this are prominent in the Bible. One is a boat—Noah's Ark—and the other is a sacred box—the Ark of the Covenant.

Babylonian Captivity (or Exile)
The period in Jewish history during which the Jews of the ancient Kingdom of Judah were captives in Babylon—conventionally 586–538 B.C.E. although some claim a date of 596 B.C.E.

B.C.
Abbreviation for "Before Christ." A system of notating time, generally used with A.D.

B.C.E.
Abbreviation for "Before the Christian Era" or "Before the Common Era." An academic and faith-neutral notation of time. Generally used with C.E.

Canon
An authoritative list of books accepted as Holy Scripture. The word is from the Latin meaning "rule" or "standard."

Catholic
With a small "c," the word means "universal." It is used this way in the Apostles' Creed. With a capital "C" the word denotes the Roman Catholic Church.

A B **C** D E F G H I J K L M N O P Q R S T U V W X Y Z

C.E.
Abbreviation for "Christian Era" or "Common Era." An academic and faith-neutral notation of time. Generally used with B.C.E.

Codex
A manuscript book especially of Scripture, classics, or ancient annals. A codex is bound like we are used to in a modern book instead of the more common scroll.

Codex Sinaiticus
A fourth-century, hand-written copy of the Greek Bible.

Concordance
An alphabetical index of all the words in a text or corpus of texts, showing every contextual occurrence of a word.

Conquest
The period of Jewish history described in the biblical book of Joshua. Many scholars believe the settlement of the Hebrews in Canaan took place over a much longer period of time and with less bloodshed than is depicted in Joshua. They would say that there was no actual "conquest" at all.

Covenant
A formal, solemn, and binding agreement.

Creationism
The doctrine or theory holding that matter, the various forms of life, and the world were created by God out of nothing in a way determined by a literal reading of Genesis.

Deuterocanonical
Of, relating to, or constituting the books of Scripture contained in the Septuagint but not in the Hebrew canon. Primarily Roman Catholic and Orthodox usage for the texts known to Jews and Protestants as the Apocrypha.

Diaspora
A scattered population originating from a single area. In this course the word refers specifically to Jews living outside of Israel.

Dispensationalism
A system of Christian belief, formalized in the nineteenth century, that divides human history into seven distinct ages or dispensations.

Evangelical
When used with a capital "E," this refers to those in Christian traditions that emphasize a high view of biblical authority, the need for personal relationship with God achieved through a conversion experience (being "born again"), and an emphasis on sharing the gospel that Jesus' death and resurrection save us from our sins. The tradition generally deemphasizes ritual and prioritizes personal experience.

Gilgamesh
A Sumerian king and hero of the Epic of Gilgamesh, which contains a story of a great flood during which a man is saved in a boat.

Hapax Legomenon (pl. Hapax Legomena)
A word or form of speech occurring only once in a document or body of work.

Hasmonean Dynasty
Those who ruled Judea in the late second century B.C.E. This represented a brief period of independence between the occupying forces of Greece and Rome and is described in the books of the Maccabees.

Hyksos
Of or relating to a Semitic dynasty that ruled Egypt from about the eighteenth to the sixteenth centuries B.C.E.

Inerrancy
Exemption from error. Infallibility.

Jerome
(ca. 347 C.E.–30 September 420 C.E.) A Roman Christian priest, confessor, theologian, and historian, who became a Doctor of the Church. Best known for his translation of the Bible into Latin (the Vulgate). Recognized by the Roman Catholic and Eastern Orthodox churches as a saint.

LXX
See Septuagint.

Mainline
Certain Protestant churches in the United States that comprised a majority of Americans from the colonial era until the early twentieth century. The group is contrasted with evangelical and fundamentalist groups. They include Congregationalists, Episcopalians, Methodists, northern Baptists, most Lutherans, and most Presbyterians, as well as some smaller denominations.

Marcion (of Sinope)
(ca. 85–160 C.E.) An early Christian bishop who believed the God of the Hebrew Scriptures to be inferior or subjugated to the God of the New Testament and developed his own canon of Scripture accordingly. He was excommunicated for his belief.

Masoretes
Groups of Jewish scribes working between the seventh and eleventh centuries C.E. They added vowel notations to the Hebrew Scriptures.

Mordecai Nathan (Rabbi)
Philosopher rabbi of the fifteenth century C.E. who wrote the first concordance to the Hebrew Bible and added numbered verse notations to the Hebrew Bible for the first time.

Orthodox
With a capital "O" referring to the Eastern Orthodox Church (and its various geographic subdivisions), the Oriental Orthodox churches (and their subdivisions), and any Western Rite Orthodox congregations allied with the above.

Ossuary
A depository, most commonly a box, for the bones (as opposed to the entire corpse) of the dead.

Pentateuch
The first five books of the Bible: Genesis, Exodus, Leviticus, Numbers, and Deuteronomy.

Pharisee
A member of a segment of Judaism of the inter-testamental period noted for strict observance of rites and ceremonies of the written law and for insistence on the validity of their own oral traditions concerning the law.

Protestant
Used here in the broadest sense of any Christian not of a Catholic or Orthodox church.

Pseudepigrapha
In biblical studies, the Pseudepigrapha are Jewish religious works written ca. 200 B.C.E.–200 C.E., which are not part of the canon of any established Jewish or Christian tradition.

Rapture
The term "rapture" is used in at least two senses in modern traditions of Christian theology: in pre-tribulationist views, in which a group of people will be "left behind," and as a synonym for the final resurrection generally.

Robert Stephanus
Protestant book printer living in France in the sixteenth century who divided the chapters of the New Testament into the verses we have today.

Septuagint or LXX
An ancient Greek translation of the Hebrew Scriptures. Translation began in the third century B.C.E. with the Pentateuch and continued for several centuries.

Stephen Langton
Theology professor in Paris and archbishop of Canterbury in the thirteenth century who first added chapter divisions to the Bible.

Supersessionism
The idea that God's covenant with Christians supersedes and therefore displaces God's covenant with Israel.

Synoptic Gospels
From the Greek meaning to "see alike," the Synoptics are Matthew, Mark, and Luke.

Testament
With a capital "T" it means either of the two main divisions of the Bible: the Old Testament or the New Testament. With a small "t" the word simply means a covenant or agreement that is formalized in writing and witnessed.

Tetragrammaton
The four consonants in Exodus 3:14 (YHWH) that comprise God's name.

Vulgate
The late fourth-century Latin translation of the Bible done by St. Jerome.

Exploring the Bible

Produced by the Massachusetts Bible Society and The Walker Group, LLC, the 28-minute video **One Book, Many Voices** will let you hear directly from scholars, clergy, and just regular folks helping you to reflect on these questions:

- **How do YOU understand the Bible?**
- **Can we trust what is in the Bible?**
- **Is there a right or wrong way to read it?**

To view the trailer and/or order a physical copy of the DVD, go to **massbible.org/DVD**. To buy or rent a streaming download, either search amazon.com for "One Book, Many Voices" or scan the QR code with your smart phone.

Help More People Explore the Bible

Your gift of $25, $50, $100, or more supports *Exploring the Bible* scholarships, study Bibles for those in need, and helps keep our training events at a reasonable cost.

$ _____   ○ One-Time Donation   ○ Recurring

_____
Name

_____
Address

_____   _____
Phone   Email

                                                   ○ Check Enclosed

_____
Credit Card Number

Mail this completed form to:
Massachusetts Bible Society
199 Herrick Rd., Newton Centre, MA 02459

_____   _____
Expiration Date   Security Code

You can also donate by calling 617.969.9404, by e-mail at dsadmin@massbible.org, or online at exploringthebible.org.

www.ingramcontent.com/pod-product-compliance
Lightning Source LLC
Chambersburg PA
CBHW080445110426
42743CB00016B/3282